To Our Readers:

The Power
Of Self Esteem

Other Books By Nathaniel Branden

The Psychology Of Self-Esteem
Breaking Free
The Disowned Self
The Psychology Of Romantic Love
What Love Asks Of Us
Honoring The Self
If You Could Hear What I Cannot Say
The Art Of Self-Discovery
How To Raise Your Self-Esteem
Judgment Day: My Years With Ayn Rand

The Power
Of Self-Esteem

Nathaniel Branden, Ph.D.

Health Communications, Inc.
Deerfield Beach, Florida

Publisher: Health Communications, Inc.
          3201 S.W. 15th Street
          Deerfield Beach, Florida 33442-8190

Cover design by Christine Clough

CONTENTS

Self-Esteem
··········
A Definition

Self-esteem is a powerful force within each one of us. It encompasses much more than that innate sense of self-worth which presumably is our human birthright — that spark that we who are psychotherapists or teachers seek to fan in those we work with. That spark is only the anteroom to self-esteem.

As you begin to read this book, I want you to know precisely what I mean when I say "self-esteem." There are many definitions which I consider misleading, less powerful or less useful than the one I propose. If self-esteem loses its precise meaning and descends to the level of a mere buzzword, it may not be taken seriously by those we are attempting to reach — the very people who need it the most.

Self-esteem is the experience that we are appropriate to life and to the requirements of life. More specifically, self-esteem is . . .

1. Confidence in our ability to think and to cope with the basic challenges of life.

2. Confidence in our right to be happy, the feeling of being worthy, deserving, entitled to assert our needs and wants and to enjoy the fruits of our efforts.

Later in this book I will refine and condense this definition, but essentially this is what I mean when I discuss the concept of self-esteem.

The Importance Of Self-Esteem
....
An Historical Perspective

All over the world today there is an awakening to the importance of self-esteem. We recognize that just as a human being cannot hope to realize his or her potential without healthy self-esteem, neither can a society whose members do not value themselves and do not trust their minds.

I want to address the issue, therefore, of what precisely "self-esteem" means, and how and why it affects our lives as profoundly as it does. Only on this foundation can we build an understanding of how the principles of self-esteem psychology can be applied in psychotherapy, and to our schools, organizations and social institutions of every kind.

Recently I found myself reflecting on the day, nearly four decades ago, when I wrote my first notes on self-esteem. It was 1954 and I was twenty-four years old, studying psychology at New York University and already

with a small private practice. The notes were not for pub-
lication but simply to help clarify my thoughts. I wrote:

> I'm beginning to think that the single most important key to
> human motivation is self-esteem. Yet no one seems to be
> writing or talking about it. What I want to understand is:
> (a) What is self-esteem?
> (b) What does it depend on?
> (c) Why does its presence or absence make such an enor-
> mous difference in people's lives?
> (d) *How can I prove it?*

When I first went to the library in search of information about self-esteem, almost none was to be found. The
indexes of books on psychology did not mention the term.
Sigmund Freud had suggested that low "self-regard" was
caused by a child's discovery that he or she could not have
sexual intercourse with the mother or father, which re-
sulted in the helpless feeling: "I can do nothing." I did not
find this persuasive or illuminating as an explanation.

Alfred Adler suggested that everyone started out with
feelings of inferiority, caused, first, by bringing some physical liability or "organ inferiority" into the world and, second, by the fact that everyone else (that is, grown-ups or
older siblings) was bigger and stronger. In other words,
our curse is that we are not born perfectly formed mature
adults. I did not find this helpful, either.

A few psychoanalysts wrote about self-esteem, but in
terms very different from my understanding of the concept, so that it was almost as if they were studying another
subject.

My first major effort to address the issues and questions self-esteem presented, *The Psychology of Self-Esteem*, was written during the 1960s and published in 1969. (I am happy and proud to say that it is now going strong in its 27th printing.)

Culturally it was only in the 1980s that self-esteem as a topic caught fire. Not only did books begin to appear in increasing numbers that made reference to the term and elaborated on it to varying extents, but more scientific studies began appearing. However, there is still no consensus about what the term means.

By the late 1980s, in the United States, one could not turn the television on without hearing things like, "When he didn't show up for our date, my self-esteem was shattered!" or "How could you let him treat you like that? Where's your self-esteem?" In a popular historical film drama about love and seduction among French aristocracy, we heard the anachronism of one character saying to another something like, "I wanted you from the first moment I saw you. My self-esteem demanded it."

If once the challenge was to gain public understanding of the importance of self-esteem, today the danger is that the idea might become trivialized. If the idea does become trivialized, the tragedy is that people will then lose the understanding of its importance.

The Importance Of A Precise Definition
. . . .

Understanding that self-esteem has an exact meaning is important. It would be unwise to dismiss definitions as mere semantics or a concern with exactitude as pedantry. The value of a precise definition is that it allows us to distinguish a particular aspect of reality from all others, so that we can think about it and work with it with clarity and focus. If we wish to know what self-esteem depends on, how to nurture it in our children, support it in schools, encourage it in organizations, strengthen it in psychotherapy, or develop it in ourselves, we need to know what precisely we are aiming at. *We are unlikely to hit a target we cannot see.*

If our idea of self-esteem is vague, the means we adopt will reflect this vagueness. If our enthusiasm for self-esteem is not matched by appropriate intellectual rigor, we run the risk not only of failing to produce worthwhile results, but also of discrediting the field.

Unfortunately, almost every writer in the field proposes a different definition of what self-esteem means. This is one of the problems with the research. Different characteristics or attributes are being measured, but all are collectively called "self-esteem." Let us examine a few representative definitions to clarify further my own approach.

Earliest Attempt To Define Self-Esteem
. . . .

The "father" of American psychology is William James, and in his *Principles of Psychology,* originally published in 1890, we find the earliest attempt I know of to define self-esteem:

I, who for the time have staked my all on being a psychologist, am mortified if others know much more psychology than I. But I am contented to wallow in the grossest ignorance of Greek. My deficiencies there give me no sense of personal humiliation at all. Had I 'pretensions' to be a linguist, it would have been just the reverse . . .. With no attempt there can be no failure; with no failure no humiliation. So our self-feeling in this world depends entirely on what we back ourselves to be and do. It is determined by the ratio of our actualities to our supposed potentialities; a fraction of which our pretensions are the denominator and the numerator our success: thus,

$$\text{Self-esteem} = \frac{\text{Success}}{\text{Pretensions}}$$

Such a fraction may be increased as well by diminishing the denominator as by increasing the numerator.

The first thing James is telling us about himself is that he bases his self-esteem on how well he compares to others in his chosen field. If no one else can match his expertise, his self-esteem is satisfied. If someone else surpasses him, his self-esteem is devastated. He is telling us that in a sense he is placing his self-esteem at the mercy of others. In his professional life, this gives him a vested interest in being surrounded by inferiors; it gives him reason to fear talent rather than welcome, admire, and take pleasure in it. This is not a formula for healthy self-esteem but a prescription for anxiety.

To tie our self-esteem to any factor outside our volitional control, such as the choices or actions of others, is to invite anguish. That so many people judge themselves just this way is their tragedy.

If "self-esteem equals success divided by pretensions," then, as James points out, self-esteem can equally be protected by increasing one's success or lowering one's pretensions. This means that a person who aspires to nothing, neither in work nor in character, and achieves it and a person of high accomplishment and high character are equals in self-esteem. I do not believe that this is an idea at which anyone could have arrived by paying attention to the real world. People with aspirations so low that they meet them mindlessly and effortlessly are not conspicuous for their psychological well-being.

How well we live up to our personal standards and values (which James unfortunately calls "pretensions") clearly has a bearing on our self-esteem. The value of James' discussion is that it draws attention to this fact. But it is a fact that cannot properly be understood in a vacuum, as if the *content* of our standards and values were irrelevant and nothing more were involved than the neutral formula James proposes. Literally, his formula is less a definition of self-esteem than a statement concerning how he believes the level of self-esteem is determined, not in some unfortunate individuals, but in everyone.

Stanley Coopersmith's Contribution
· · · · · · · · · · · ·

One of the best books written on self-esteem is Stanley Coopersmith's *The Antecedents of Self-Esteem*. His research on the contribution of parents remains invaluable. He writes:

> By self-esteem we refer to the evaluation which the individual makes and customarily maintains with regard to himself. It expresses an attitude of approval or disapproval, and indicates the extent to which the individual believes himself to be capable, significant, successful, and worthy. In short, self-esteem is a *personal* judgment of worthiness that is expressed in the attitudes the individual holds toward himself.

Relative to James, this formulation represents a great step forward. It speaks much more directly to what our experience of self-esteem is. Yet there are questions it raises and leaves unanswered.

"Capable" of what? All of us are capable in some areas and not in others. Capable relative to whatever we undertake? Then must any lack of adequate competence diminish self-esteem? I do not think Coopersmith would want to suggest this, but the implication is left hanging.

"Significant" — what does this mean? Significant in what way? Significant in the eyes of others? Which others? Significant by what standards?

"Successful" — does this mean worldly success? Financial success? Career success? Social success? Success with regard to what? Note he is not saying that self-esteem contains the idea that success (in principle) is *appropriate;* he is saying that self-esteem contains the idea of *seeing oneself as successful* — which is entirely different and troublesome in its implications.

"Worthy" — of what? Happiness? Money? Love? Anything the individual desires? My sense is that Coopersmith would mean by "worthy" pretty much what I spell out in my own definition in the preface to this book, but he does not say so.

More Recent Attempts To Define Self-Esteem

Another definition is offered by Richard L. Bednar, M. Gawain Wells and Scott R. Peterson in their book *Self-Esteem: Paradoxes and Innovations in Clinical Theory and Practice:*

> Parenthetically, we define self-esteem as a subjective and endearing sense of realistic self-approval. It reflects how the individual views and values the self at the most fundamental levels of psychological experiencing . . .. Fundamentally, then, self-esteem is an enduring and affective sense of personal value based on accurate self-perception.

"Approval" — with regard to what? Everything about the self from physical appearance to actions to intellectual functioning? We are not told. "Views and values the self" — with regard to what issues or criteria? "An enduring and affective sense of personal value" — what does this mean? On the other hand, what I like in this formulation is the observation that genuine self-esteem is reality based.

One of the most widely publicized definitions of self-esteem is given in *Toward A State of Esteem: The Final Report of the California Task Force To Promote Self and Personal and Social Responsibility:*

Self-esteem is defined as: Appreciating my own worth and importance and having the character to be accountable for myself and to act responsibly toward others.

In this definition, we find the same lack of specificity as in the other definitions — "worth and importance" *with regard to what?*

There is another problem with the Task Force statement: inserting into the definition what is obviously meant to be a basic *source* of healthy self-esteem (that is, being accountable for oneself and acting responsibly toward others). A definition of a psychological state is meant to tell us what a state *is*, not how one gets there. Did the people who offered this definition want us to understand that if we don't act responsibly toward others, we won't possess healthy self-esteem? If so, they are probably right, but is that part of the definition — or is it a different issue? (Almost certainly such a definition is influenced by "political" rather than scientific considerations — to reassure people that champions of self-esteem are not fostering petty, irresponsible "selfishness.")

Finally there are those in the self-esteem movement who announce that "self-esteem means 'I am capable and lovable.'"

Again we must ask, "'Capable' of what?" I am a great skier, a brilliant lawyer, and a first-rate chef. However, I don't feel competent to assess independently the moral values my mother taught me. I feel, Who am I to know? In such a case, am I "capable"? Do I have self-esteem?

As to "lovable" — yes, feeling lovable is one of the characteristics of healthy self-esteem. So is feeling worthy

of happiness and success. Is feeling lovable more important? Evidently, since the other two items are not mentioned. *By what reasoning?*

Am I suggesting that the definition of self-esteem I offer
is written in stone and can never be improved on? Not at
all. Definitions are contextual; they relate to a given level
of knowledge; as knowledge grows, definitions tend to
become more precise. I may find a better, clearer, more
exact way to capture the essence of the concept during my
lifetime. Or someone else may. But within the context of
the knowledge we now possess, I can think of no alternative formulation that identifies with more precision the
unique aspect of human experience we call self-esteem.

The Purpose Of This Book
. . . .

The purpose of this book is not to address exhaustively
the great issue of what we can do to heal or rebuild a
damaged self-esteem, but, more fundamentally, to explore
what self-esteem *is.*

This is the necessary starting point. While there is a
good deal of talk about the subject these days, there is no
shared understanding of the meaning of self-esteem or
the reasons why it is so important to our well-being.
These are the basic issues I write about here.

In Chapter 1, I invite the reader to look at the powerful
role self-esteem plays for all of us in the key choices and
decisions that shape our lives. I explore what self-esteem

means, develop a definition of the term and give my reasons for it for the purpose of clarifying what I believe are misconceptions and discuss why the need for self-esteem arises in our species.

In Chapter 2, I describe what good self-esteem looks like and indicate the mental operations on which healthy self-esteem depends. In Chapter 3, I point out the difference between pseudo-self-esteem and authentic self-esteem. The first three chapters are adapted from a talk I gave in Asker/Oslo, Norway, at the First International Conference on Self-Esteem in the summer of 1990.

In Chapter 4, I offer a number of observations about the sources of healthy self-esteem, insofar as it depends on our own choices and behavior.

In Chapter 5, I discuss the application of self-esteem principles to the workplace.

Finally in Chapter 6, I make recommendations for further study. If this is the first book you have read on self-esteem, Chapter 6 suggests where you might wish to go next. I hope you will wish to go further and learn more about self-esteem because, as I say in Chapter 1, of all the judgments we pass in life, none is more important than the judgment we pass on ourselves.

Self-concept is destiny.

What Is Self-Esteem?

....

Most of us are children of dysfunctional families.

I do not mean that most of us had alcoholic parents or were sexually or otherwise abused or that we grew up in an atmosphere of physical violence. I mean that most of us grew up in homes characterized by conflicting signals, denials of reality, parental lying, and lack of adequate respect for our mind and person. I am speaking of the *average* home.

I recall discussing this issue one day with the distinguished family therapist Virginia Satir, who offered an exquisite and appalling example of the kind of craziness with which so many of us grew up.

Imagine, she said, a scene among a child, a mother, and a father.

Seeing a look of unhappiness on the mother's face, the child asks, "What's the matter, Mommy? You look sad."

Mother answers, her voice tight and constricted, "Nothing's the matter. I am fine."

Then Father says angrily, "Don't upset your mother!"

The child looks back and forth between mother and father, utterly bewildered, unable to understand the rebuke. She begins to weep. The mother cries to Father, "Now look what you've done!"

I like this story because of its ordinariness. Let us consider it more closely.

The child correctly perceives that something is troubling Mother and responds appropriately. Mother acts by invalidating the child's (correct) perception of reality; she lies. Perhaps Mother does so out of the misguided desire to "protect" her child or perhaps because she herself does not know how to handle her unhappiness. If she had said, "Yes, Mommy is feeling a little sad right now; thank you for noticing," she would have validated the child's perception. By acknowledging her own unhappiness simply and openly, she would have reinforced the child's compassion and taught something important concerning a healthy attitude toward pain; she would have de-catastrophized the pain.

Father, perhaps to "protect" Mother or perhaps out of guilt because Mother's sadness concerns him, rebukes the child, thus adding to the incomprehensibility of the situation. If the mother is not sad, why would a simple inquiry be upsetting? If she is sad, why is it wrong to ask about it and why is Mommy lying? Now, to confound the child still

more, Mother screams at Father, rebuking him for re-
proaching their child. Contradictions compounded; incongruities on top of incongruities. How is the child to make
sense of the situation?

The child may run outside, frantically looking for something to do or someone to play with, seeking to erase all
memory of the incident as quickly as possible, repressing
feelings and perceptions. And if the child flees into uncon-
sciousness to escape the terrifying sense of being trapped
in a nightmare, do we blame her well-meaning parents for
behaving in ways that encourage her to feel that sight is
dangerous and that there is safety in blindness?

A Story Without Villains
. . . .

An unexceptional story without villains. No one is likely
to imagine that the parents are motivated by destructive
intentions. But in choosing to deny simple reality, they
give the child the impression that she exists in an incomprehensible world where perception is untrustworthy and
thought is futile. Multiply that incident by a thousand
more or less like it, none of which the child is likely to
remember in later years, but all of which will almost certainly have a cumulative impact on the child's development.
(Are not most of us survivors of such experiences?)

If the child does draw the conclusion that her mind is
impotent, or that its potency is doubtful, how can a good
self-esteem develop? And without it, how will she face
life?

Complex Factors Determine Our Self-Esteem
• • • • • • • • • • • •

I do not wish to imply that how our parents treat us determines the level of our self-esteem. The matter is more complex than that. We have a decisive role of our own to play. The notion that we are merely pawns shaped and determined by our environment cannot be supported scientifically or philosophically. We are causal agents in our own right; active contestants in the drama of our lives; originators and not merely reactors or responders.

Clearly, however, the family environment can have a profound impact for good or for ill. Parents can nurture self-trust and self-respect or place appalling roadblocks in the way of learning such attitudes. They can convey that they believe in their child's competence and goodness or they can convey the opposite. They can create an environment in which the child feels safe and secure or they can create an environment of terror. They can support the emergence of healthy self-esteem or they can do everything conceivable to subvert it.

Obstacles To The Growth Of Self-Esteem
• • • • • • • • • • • •

Parents throw up severe obstacles to the growth of a child's self-esteem when they . . .

• Convey that the child is not "enough."

• Chastise the child for expressing "unacceptable" feelings.

- Ridicule or humiliate the child.

- Convey that the child's thoughts or feelings have no value or importance.

- Attempt to control the child by shame or guilt.

- Over-protect the child and consequently obstruct normal learning and increasing self-reliance.

- Raise a child with no rules at all, and thus no supporting structure, or else rules that are contradictory, bewildering, undiscussable, and oppressive, in either case inhibiting normal growth.

- Deny a child's perception of reality and implicitly encourage the child to doubt his or her mind.

- Treat evident facts as unreal, thus shaking the child's sense of rationality — for example, when an alcoholic father stumbles to the dinner table, misses the chair, and falls to the floor as the mother goes on eating or talking as if nothing had happened.

- Terrorize a child with physical violence or the threat of it, thus instilling acute fear as an enduring characteristic at the child's core.

- Treat a child as a sexual object.

- Teach that the child is bad, unworthy, or sinful by nature.

Today millions of men and women who have come out of such childhood experiences are searching for ways to heal their wounds. They recognize that they have entered adult life with a liability — a deficit of self-esteem. Whatever words they use to describe the problem, they know they suffer from some nameless sense of not being "enough," or some haunting emotion of shame or guilt, or a generalized self-distrust, or a diffusive feeling of unworthiness. They sense their lack *even if they do not know what precisely self-esteem is*, let alone how to nurture and strengthen it within themselves.

A Definition Of Self-Esteem
. . . .

We who are psychotherapists or teachers seek to fan a spark in those we work with — that innate sense of self-worth that presumably is our human birthright. But that spark is only the anteroom to self-esteem. If we are to do justice to those we work with, we need to help them develop that sense of self-worth into the full experience of self-esteem.

Self-esteem is the experience that we are appropriate to life and to the requirements of life. More specifically, self-esteem is . . .

1. Confidence in our ability to think and to cope with the challenges of life.

2. Confidence in our right to be happy, the feeling of being worthy, deserving, entitled to assert our needs and wants and to enjoy the fruits of our efforts.

A Powerful Human Need

• • • • • • • • • • •

Self-esteem is a powerful human need. It is a basic human need that makes an essential contribution to the life process; it is indispensable to normal and healthy development; it has survival value.

Lacking positive self-esteem, our psychological growth is stunted. Positive self-esteem operates as, in effect, *the immune system of consciousness*, providing resistance, strength, and a capacity for regeneration. When self-esteem is low, our resilience in the face of life's adversities is diminished. We crumble before vicissitudes that a healthier sense of self could vanquish. We tend to be more influenced by the desire to avoid pain than to experience joy. Negatives have more power over us than positives.

Addiction And Self-Esteem

• • • • • • • • • • •

These observations help us to understand addictions. When we become addicted to alcohol or drugs or destructive relationships, the unconscious intention is invariably to ameliorate anxiety and pain. What we become addicted to are tranquilizers and anodynes. The "enemies" we are trying to escape are fear and pain. When the means we have chosen do not work and make our problems worse, we are driven to take more and more of the poison that is killing us.

Addicts are not *less* fearful than other human beings, they are *more* fearful. Their pain is not milder, it is more severe. We cannot drink or drug our way into self-esteem anymore than we can buy happiness with toxic relationships. We do not attain self-esteem by practices that evoke self-hatred.

If we do not believe in ourselves — neither in our efficacy nor in our goodness — the universe is a frightening place.

Valuing Ourselves
. . . .

This does not mean that we are necessarily incapable of achieving any real values. Some of us may have the talent and drive to achieve a great deal, in spite of a poor self-concept — like the highly productive workaholic who is driven to prove his worth to, say, a father who predicted he would amount to nothing. But it does mean that we will be less effective — less creative — than we have the power to be; and it means that we will be crippled in our ability to find joy in our achievements. Nothing we do will ever feel like "enough."

If we do have realistic confidence in our mind and value, if we feel secure within ourselves, we tend to experience the world as open to us and to respond appropriately to challenges and opportunities. Self-esteem empowers, energizes, motivates. It inspires us to achieve and allows us to take pleasure and pride in our achievements. It allows us to experience satisfaction.

In their enthusiasm, some writers today seem to suggest that a healthy sense of self-value is all we need to assure happiness and success. The matter is more complex than that.

We have more than one need, and there is no single solution to all the problems of our existence. A well-developed sense of self is a necessary condition of our well-being but not a sufficient condition. Its presence does not guarantee fulfillment, but its lack guarantees some measure of anxiety, frustration, despair.

Self-esteem proclaims itself as a need by virtue of the fact that its (relative) absence impairs our ability to function. This is why we say it has survival value.

And never more so than today. We have reached a moment in history when self-esteem, which has always been a supremely important psychological need, has also become a supremely important economic need — an attribute imperative for adaptiveness to an increasingly complex, challenging, and competitive world.

Psychological Resources For The Future
. . . .

The shift from a manufacturing society to an information society, the shift from physical labor to mind-work as the dominant employee activity, and the emergence of a global economy characterized by rapid change, accelerating scientific and technological breakthroughs, and an unprecedented level of competitiveness, create demands for higher levels of education and training than were required of previous generations. Everyone acquainted with busi-

ness culture knows this. But what is not equally understood is that these developments also create new demands
on our psychological resources.

Specifically, these developments ask for a greater capacity for innovation, self-management, personal responsibility, and self-direction. This is asked not just "at the
top," but at every level of a business enterprise, from
senior management to first-line supervisors and even to
entry-level personnel.

A modern business can no longer be run by a few
people who think and a great many people who do what
they are told (the traditional military, command-and-con-
trol model). Today organizations need not only an un-
precedentedly higher level of knowledge and skill among
all those who participate, but also a higher level of personal autonomy, self-reliance, self-trust, and the capacity
to exercise initiative — in a word, self-esteem. This means
that people possessing a decent level of self-esteem are
now needed economically in large numbers. Historically
this is a new phenomenon. (The importance of self-esteem
in the workplace is discussed at length in Chapter 4.)

Intelligent Choices Require Self-Esteem
· · · · · · · · · · · ·

In a world where there are more choices and options
than ever before, and frontiers of limitless possibilities
face us in whatever direction we look, we require a higher
level of personal autonomy. This means a greater need to

exercise independent judgment, to cultivate our own resources, and to take responsibility for the choices, values, and actions that shape our lives; a greater need for self-trust and self-reliance; a greater need for a reality-based belief in ourselves.

The greater the number of choices and decisions we need to make at a conscious level, the more urgent our need for self-esteem.

To the extent that we are confident in the efficacy of our minds — confident of our ability to think, learn, understand — we tend to persevere when faced with difficult or complex challenges. Persevering, we tend to succeed more often than we fail, thus confirming and reinforcing our sense of efficacy. To the extent that we doubt the efficacy of our minds and lack confidence in our thinking, we tend not to persevere but to give up. Giving up, we fail more often than we succeed, thus confirming and reinforcing our negative self-assessment.

High self-esteem seeks the stimulation of demanding goals, and reaching demanding goals nurtures good self-esteem. Low self-esteem seeks the safety of the familiar and undemanding, and confining oneself to the familiar and undemanding serves to weaken self-esteem.

The higher our self-esteem, the better equipped we are to cope with adversity in our careers or in our personal lives, the quicker we are to pick ourselves up after a fall, the more energy we have to begin anew.

The higher our self-esteem, the more ambitious we tend to be, not necessarily in a career or financial sense, but in terms of what we hope to experience in life — emotionally, creatively, spiritually. The lower our self-esteem, the less we aspire to, and the less we are likely to achieve. Either path tends to be self-reinforcing and self-perpetuating.

The higher our self-esteem, the more disposed we are to form nourishing rather than toxic relationships. Like is drawn to like, health is attracted to health, and vitality and expansiveness in others are naturally more appealing to people of good self-esteem than are emptiness and dependency.

Attraction To Those Whose Self-Esteem Level Matches Our Own
. . . .

An important principle of human relationships is that we tend to feel most comfortable, most "at home," with people whose self-esteem level resembles our own. High self-esteem individuals tend to be drawn to high self-esteem individuals. Medium self-esteem individuals are typically attracted to medium self-esteem individuals. Low self-esteem seeks low self-esteem in others. The most disastrous relationships are those between two persons both of whom think poorly of themselves; the union of two abysses does not produce a height.

I am thinking of a woman I once treated who grew up feeling she was "bad" and undeserving of kindness, respect or happiness. Predictably, she married a man who "knew" he was unlovable and felt consumed by self-hatred. He protected himself by being cruel to others before they could be cruel to him. She did not complain about his abuse, since she "knew" that abuse was her destiny. He was not surprised by her increasing withdrawal and remoteness from him, since he "knew" no one could ever love him.

They had spent twenty years of torture together, "proving" how right they were about themselves and about life. When I commented to the wife that she had not known much happiness, she looked at me astonished and said, "Are people ever really happy?"

The higher our self-esteem, the more inclined we are to treat others with respect, benevolence, good will, and fairness — since we do not tend to perceive them as a threat, and since self-respect is the foundation of respect for others.

The Time-Bomb Of Poor Self-Esteem

. . . .

While an inadequate self-esteem can severely limit an individual's aspirations and accomplishments, the consequences of the problem need not be so obvious. Sometimes the consequences show up in more indirect ways. The time-bomb of a poor self-concept may tick silently for years while an individual, driven by a passion for success and exercising genuine ability, may rise higher and higher in his profession. Then, without real necessity, he starts cutting corners, morally and/or legally, in his eagerness to provide more lavish demonstrations of his mastery. Then he commits more flagrant offenses still, telling himself that he is "beyond good and evil," as if challenging the fates to bring him down. Only at the end, when his life and career explode in disgrace and ruin, can we see for how many years he has been moving relentlessly toward the final act of an unconscious lifescript he may have begun writing at the age of three.

Self-Efficacy And Self-Respect

. . . .

Self-esteem has two interrelated aspects:

1. A sense of personal efficacy (self-efficacy)

2. A sense of personal worth (self-respect).

As a fully realized psychological experience, it is the integrated sum of these two aspects.

Self-efficacy means confidence in the functioning of my mind, in my ability to think, in the processes by which I judge, choose, decide; confidence in my ability to understand the facts of reality that fall within the sphere of my interests and needs; cognitive self-trust; cognitive self-reliance.

Self-respect means assurance of my value; an affirmative attitude toward my right to live and to be happy; comfort in appropriately asserting my thoughts, wants, and needs; the feeling that joy is my natural birthright.

Consider that if an individual felt inadequate to face the challenges of life, if an individual lacked fundamental self-trust, confidence in his or her mind, we would recognize the presence of a self-esteem deficiency, no matter what other assets he or she possessed. Or if an individual lacked a basic sense of self-respect, felt unworthy or undeserving of the love or respect of others, unentitled to happiness, fearful of asserting thoughts, wants, or needs — again we would recognize a self-esteem deficiency, no matter what other positive attributes he or she exhibited.

The Dual Pillars Of Self-Esteem
. . . .

Self-efficacy and self-respect are the dual pillars of healthy self-esteem. Lacking either one, self-esteem is impaired. They are the defining characteristics of the term because of their fundamentality. They represent not derivative or secondary meanings of self-esteem but its essence.

The experience of *self-efficacy* generates the sense of control over one's life that we associate with psychological well-being, the sense of being at the vital center of one's existence — as contrasted with being a passive spectator and a victim of events.

The experience of *self-respect* makes possible a benevolent, non-neurotic sense of community with other individuals, the fellowship of independence and mutual regard — as contrasted with either alienated estrangement from the human race, on the one hand, or mindless submergence into the tribe, on the other.

Within a given person, there will be inevitable fluctuations in self-esteem levels, much as there are fluctuations in all psychological states. We need to think in terms of a person's *average level of self-esteem*.

How Do We Experience Our Self-Esteem?

. . . .

While we sometimes speak of self-esteem as a conviction about oneself, it is more accurate to speak of a disposition to experience oneself a particular way. What way? To recapitulate:

1. As fundamentally competent to cope with the challenges of life; thus, trust in one's mind and its processes; *self-efficacy*.

2. As worthy of success and happiness; thus, the perception of oneself as someone to whom achievement, success, respect, friendship and love, are appropriate; *self-respect*.

A Formal Definition Of Self-Esteem

. . . .

To sum up in a formal definition: *Self-esteem is the disposition to experience oneself as competent to cope with the challenges of life and as deserving of happiness.*

Note that this definition does not specify the childhood environmental influences that support healthy self-esteem (e.g., physical safety, nurturing, etc.), nor the later internal generators (e.g., the practice of living consciously, self-responsibly, etc.), nor emotional or behavioral consequences (e.g., compassion, willingness to be accountable, etc.). *It merely identifies what the self-evaluation concerns and consists of.*

Am I suggesting that the definition of self-esteem I offer is written in stone and can never be improved on? Not at all. Definitions are contextual. They relate to a given level of knowledge; as knowledge grows, definitions tend to become more precise. I may find a better, clearer, more exact way to capture the essence of the concept during my lifetime. Or someone else may. But within the context of the knowledge we now possess, I can think of no alternative formulation that identifies with more precision the unique aspect of human experience we call self-esteem.

The concept of "competence" as used in my definition is metaphysical, not "Western." That is, it pertains to the very nature of things — to our fundamental relationship to reality. It is not the product of a particular cultural "value bias." There is no society on earth, no society even conceivable, whose members do not face the challenges of fulfilling their needs — who do not face the challenges of appropriate adaptation to nature and to the world of human beings. The idea of efficacy in this fundamental sense (which includes competence in human relationships) is not a "Western artifact," as I have heard suggested.

We delude ourselves if we imagine there is any culture or society in which we will not have to face the challenge of making ourselves appropriate to life.

2

Why Do We Need Self-Esteem?

. . . .

T o understand self-esteem, we must consider: Why does the need for it arise?

The question of the efficacy of their consciousness or the worthiness of their beings does not exist for lower animals. But human beings wonder: Can I trust my mind? Am I competent to think? Am I adequate? Am I enough? Am I a good person? Do I have integrity — that is, is there congruence between my ideals and my practice? Am I worthy of respect, love, success, happiness? It is not self-evident why such questions should even occur.

Our need of self-esteem is the result of two basic facts, both intrinsic to our species. The first is that we depend for our survival and our successful mastery of the environment on the appropriate use of our consciousness. Our lives and well-being depend on our ability to think. The second is that the right use of our consciousness is not automatic, is not "wired in" by nature. In the regulating of its activity, there is a crucial element of choice — therefore, of personal responsibility.

The Mind Is The Basic Tool Of Survival
. . . .

Like every other species capable of awareness, we depend for our survival and well-being on the guidance of our distinctive form of consciousness, the form uniquely human, our conceptual faculty — the faculty of abstraction, generalization, and integration.

This form of consciousness is what I understand by the term *mind*. Its essence is our ability to reason, which means to grasp relationships. Our lives and well-being depend on the appropriate exercise of our minds.

Mind is more than immediate explicit awareness. It is a complex architecture of structures and processes. It includes more than the verbal, linear, analytic processes popularly, if misleadingly, described sometimes as "left-brain" activity. It includes the totality of mental life, including the subconscious, the intuitive, the symbolic, all that which sometimes is associated with the "right brain." Mind is all that by means of which we reach out to and apprehend the world.

The Process Of Thought
• • • • • • • • • • •

To learn to grow food, to construct a bridge, to harness electricity, to grasp the healing possibilities of some substance, to allocate resources so as to maximize productivity, to see wealth-producing possibilities where they had not been seen before, to conduct a scientific experiment, to create — all require a process of thought. To respond appropriately to the complaints of a child or a spouse, to recognize that there is a disparity between our behavior and our professed feelings, to discover how to deal with hurt and anger in ways that will heal rather than destroy — require a process of thought.

Even to know when to abandon conscious efforts at problem-solving and turn the task over to the subconscious, to know when to allow conscious thinking to stop, or when to attend more closely to feelings or intuition (subconscious perceptions or integrations) — require a process of thought, a process of rational connection.

To Think Or Not To Think: A Choice
• • • • • • • • • • •

The problem and the challenge is that, although thinking is a necessity of successful existence, we are not programmed to think automatically. We have a choice.

We are not responsible for controlling the activities of our heart, lungs, liver or kidneys. They are all part of the body's self-regulating system (although we are beginning to learn that some measure of control of these activities may be possible to us). Nor are we obliged to supervise the homeostatic processes by which, for instance, a more or less constant temperature is maintained. Nature has designed the organs and systems of our bodies to function automatically in the service of our life without our volitional intervention. But our minds operate differently.

Our minds do not pump knowledge as our hearts pump blood, when and as needed. Our minds do not automatically guide us to act on our best, most rational and informed understanding, even when such understanding would clearly be beneficial. We do not begin to think "instinctively" merely because non-thinking, in a given situation, has become dangerous to us.

Consciousness does not "reflexly" expand in the face of the new and unfamiliar; sometimes we contract it instead. Nature has given us an extraordinary responsibility: the option of turning the searchlight of consciousness brighter or dimmer. This is the option of seeking awareness or not bothering to seek it or actively avoiding it, the option of thinking or not thinking. This is the root of our freedom and our responsibility.

We Can Make Rational Or Irrational Choices
. . . .

We are the one species who can formulate a vision of what values are worth pursuing — and then pursue the opposite. We can decide that a given course of action is rational, moral, and wise — and then suspend consciousness and proceed to do something else. We are able to monitor our behavior and ask if it is consistent with our knowledge, convictions, and ideals — and we are also able to evade asking that question. The option of thinking or not thinking.

If I have reason to know that alcohol is dangerous to me and I nonetheless take a drink, I must first turn down the light of consciousness. If I know that cocaine has cost me my last three jobs and I nonetheless choose to take a snort, I must first blank out my knowledge, must refuse to see what I see and know what I know. I recognize that I am in a relationship that is destructive of my dignity, ruinous for my self-esteem, and dangerous to my physical well-being. If I nonetheless choose to remain in it, I must drown out awareness, fog my brain, and make myself functionally stupid. Self-destruction is an act best performed in the dark.

Our Choices Affect Our Self-Esteem
. . . .

The choices we make concerning the operations of our consciousness have enormous ramifications for our lives in general and our self-esteem in particular. Consider the impact on our lives and on our sense of self entailed by the following options:

Focusing versus nonfocusing.

Thinking versus nonthinking.

Awareness versus unawareness.

Clarity versus obscurity or vagueness.

Respect for reality versus avoidance of reality.

Respect for facts versus indifference to facts.

Respect for truth versus rejection of truth.

Perseverance in the effort to understand versus abandonment of the effort.

Loyalty in action to our professed convictions versus disloyalty — the issue of integrity.

Honesty with self versus dishonesty.

Self-confrontation versus self-avoidance.

Receptivity to new knowledge versus closed-mindedness.

Willingness to see and correct errors versus perseverance in error.

Concern with congruence versus disregard of contradictions.

Reason versus irrationalism; respect for logic, consistency, coherence, and evidence versus disregard or defiance of.

Loyalty to the responsibility of consciousness versus betrayal of that responsibility.

If one wishes to understand the foundations of genuine self-esteem, this list is a good place to begin.

No one could seriously suggest that our sense of our competence to cope with the challenge of life or our sense of our goodness could remain unaffected, over time, by the pattern of our choices in regard to the above options.

Consciousness, Responsibility, Moral Choices

The point is not that our self-esteem "should" be affected by the choices we make, but rather that by our natures it *must* be affected. If we develop habit patterns that cripple or incapacitate us for effective functioning, and that cause us to distrust ourselves, it would be irrational to suggest that we "should" go on feeling just as efficacious and worthy as we would feel if our choices had been better. This would imply that our actions have or should have nothing to do with how we feel about ourselves. It is one thing to caution against identifying oneself with a particular behavior; it is another to assert that there should be *no* connection between self-assessment and behavior.

A disservice is done to people if they are offered "feel good" notions of self-esteem that divorce it from questions of consciousness, responsibility, or moral choice.

It is the fact that we have choices such as I have described, that we are confronted by options encountered nowhere else in nature, that we are the one species able to betray and act against our means of survival, that creates our need for self-esteem — which is the need to know that we are functioning as our life and well-being require.

3

Self-Esteem
And
Achievement

S elf-esteem is not a free gift that we need only claim. Its possession over time represents an achievement.

To qualify as authentic self-esteem, the experience I am describing must be reality based. It is more than simply a matter of "feeling good about oneself" — a state that, at least temporarily, can be induced in any number of ways, from having a pleasant sexual encounter to buying a new outfit to receiving a compliment to ingesting certain drugs. Genuine self-efficacy and self-respect ask more of us than this.

In *Time* (February 5, 1990), an article appeared that stated:

A standardized math test was given to 13-year-olds in six countries last year. Koreans did the best, Americans did the worst, coming in behind Spain, Ireland, and Canada. Now the bad news. Besides being shown triangles and equations, the kids were shown the statement "I am good at mathematics."

Americans were No.1, with an impressive 68% in agreement. American students may not know their math, but they have evidently absorbed the lessons of the newly fashionable self-esteem curriculum wherein kids are taught to feel good about themselves.

Within the limits of this naive and primitive understanding of self-esteem, the criticisms of "self-esteem curriculums" the author of this article goes on to make are justified. Therefore, when I write of self-efficacy or self-respect, I do so in the context of reality, not of feelings generated out of wishes or affirmations. One of the characteristics of people with healthy self-esteem is that they tend to assess their abilities and accomplishments realistically, neither denying nor exaggerating them.

Might a student do poorly in school and yet have good self-esteem? Of course. There are any number of reasons why a particular boy or girl might not do well scholastically, including lack of adequate challenge and stimulation. Grades are hardly a reliable indicator of a given individual's self-efficacy and self-respect. But rationally self-esteeming students do not delude themselves that they are doing well when they are doing poorly.

Schools should indeed be concerned to introduce self-esteem principles and practices into their curricula, and there are some excellent programs now in place. But we do not serve the healthy development of young people when we convey that self-esteem may be achieved by reciting "I am special" every day, or by stroking one's own face while saying "I love me," or by identifying self-worth with membership in a particular group ("ethnic pride") rather than with personal character.

On this last point, let us remember that self-esteem pertains to that which is open to our volitional choice. It cannot properly be a function of the family we were born into, or our race, or the color of our skin, or the achievements of our ancestors. These are values people sometimes cling to in order to avoid responsibility for achieving authentic self-esteem. They are sources of what, below, I call "pseudo-self-esteem." Can one ever take legitimate pleasure in any of these values? Of course. Can they ever provide temporary support for fragile, growing egos? Probably. But they are not substitutes for consciousness, responsibility, or integrity. They are not sources of self-efficacy and self-respect. They can, however, become sources of self-delusion.

But Is It Authentic?
. . . .

Sometimes we see people who enjoy worldly success, or are widely esteemed, and who have a public veneer of assurance, yet are deeply dissatisfied, anxious, or depressed. They may project the appearance of self-esteem, but do not possess the reality. How might we understand them?

Let us begin with the observation that to the extent that we fail to develop authentic self-esteem, the consequences are varying degrees of anxiety, insecurity, self-doubt. This is the sense of being, in effect, inappropriate to existence (although no one thinks of it in these terms; instead, one might feel something is wrong with me). This state is extremely painful. And because it is painful, we are motivated to evade it, to deny our fears, rationalize our behavior, and fake a self-esteem we do not possess. We may develop what I have termed pseudo-self-esteem.

Pseudo-self-esteem is the illusion of self-efficacy and self-respect without the reality. It is a nonrational, self-protective device to diminish anxiety and to provide a spurious sense of security — to assuage our need for authentic self-esteem while allowing the real causes of its lack to be evaded. It is based on values that may be appropriate or inappropriate but that in either case are not intrinsically related to that which genuine self-efficacy and self-respect require.

For example, instead of seeking self-esteem through consciousness, responsibility, and integrity, we may seek it through popularity, prestige, material acquisitions, or sexual exploits. Instead of valuing personal authenticity, we may value belonging to the right clubs, or the right church, or the right political party. Instead of practicing appropriate self-assertion, we may practice blind loyalty to our particular group. Instead of seeking self-respect through honesty, we may seek it through philanthropy (I must be a good person, I do "good works"). Instead of striving for the power of competence, we may pursue the "power" of manipulating or controlling other people.

The possibilities for self-deception are almost endless — all the blind alleys down which we can lose ourselves, not realizing that what we desire cannot be purchased with counterfeit currency.

Self-esteem is an intimate experience; it resides in the core of my being. It is what I think and feel about myself, not what someone else thinks or feels about me. This simple fact can hardly be over-stressed.

I can be loved by my family, my mate, and my friends, and yet not love myself. I can be admired by my associates yet regard myself as worthless. I can project an image of assurance and poise that fools virtually everyone and yet secretly tremble with a sense of my inadequacy.

I can fulfill the expectations of others and yet fail my own; I can win every honor, yet feel I have accomplished nothing; I can be adored by millions and yet wake up each morning with a sickening sense of fraudulence and emptiness.

To attain "success" without attaining positive self-esteem is to be condemned to feeling like an impostor anxiously awaiting exposure.

Acclaim Is Not Self-Esteem
. . . .

The acclaim of others does not create our self-esteem. Neither do knowledge, skills, material possessions, marriage, parenthood, philanthropic endeavors, sexual conquests, or face lifts. These things can sometimes make us feel better about ourselves temporarily, or more comfortable in particular situations. But comfort is not self-esteem.

Unfortunately, teachers of self-esteem are no less impervious to the worship of false gods than anyone else. I recall listening to a lecture by a man who conducts self-esteem seminars. He announced that one of the very best ways to raise our self-esteem is to surround ourselves with people who think highly of us. I thought of the nightmare of low self-esteem in persons surrounded by praise and adulation — like rock stars who have no idea how they got where they are and who cannot survive a day without drugs. I thought of the futility of telling a person of low self-esteem, who feels lucky if he or she is accepted by anyone, that the way to raise self-esteem is to seek the company only of admirers.

Clearly it is wiser to seek companions who are the friends of one's self-esteem rather than its enemies. Nurturing relationships are preferable to toxic ones. But to look to others as a primary source of our self-esteem is dangerous: first, because it doesn't work; and second, because we run the risk of becoming approval addicts, which is deadly to mental and emotional well-being.

I do not wish to suggest that a psychologically healthy person is unaffected by the feedback he or she receives from others. We are social beings and certainly others contribute to our self-perceptions. But there are gigantic differences among people in the relative importance to their self-esteem of the feedback they receive — persons for whom it is almost the only factor of importance and persons for whom the importance is a good deal less. This is merely another way of saying there are gigantic differences among people in the degree of their autonomy.

Having worked for over thirty years with persons who are unhappily preoccupied with the opinions of others, I am persuaded that the most effective means of liberation is by raising the level of consciousness one brings to one's own experience; the more one turns up the volume on one's inner signals, the more external signals tend to recede into proper balance. This entails, as I wrote in *Honoring The Self*, learning to listen to the body, learning to listen to the emotions, learning to think for oneself.

Authentic Pride
. . . .

If self-esteem pertains to the experience of our fundamental competence and value, *pride* pertains to the more explicitly conscious pleasure we take in ourselves because of our actions and achievements. Self-esteem contemplates what needs to be done and says "I can." Pride contemplates what has been accomplished and says "I did."

Authentic pride has nothing in common with bragging, boasting, or arrogance. It comes from an opposite root. Not emptiness but satisfaction is its wellspring. It is not out to "prove" but to enjoy.

Pride is the emotional reward of achievement. It is not a vice to be overcome, but a value to be attained. Does achievement always result in pride? Not necessarily, as the following story illustrates.

The head of a medium-sized company consulted me because, he said, although he had made a great success of his business, he was depressed and unhappy and could not understand why. We discovered that what he had always wanted to be was a research scientist but that he had abandoned that desire in deference to his parents who pushed him toward a career in business. Not only was he unable to feel more than the most superficial kind of pride in his accomplishments, but he was wounded in his self-esteem.

The reason was not difficult to identify. In the most important issue of his life he had surrendered his mind and values to the wishes of others, out of the wish to be "loved" and to "belong." Clearly a still earlier self-esteem problem motivated such a capitulation.

His depression reflected a lifetime of performing brilliantly while ignoring his deepest needs. While he operated within that framework, pride and satisfaction were beyond his reach. Until he was willing to challenge that framework, and to face the fear of doing so, no solution was possible.

This is an important point to understand because we sometimes hear people say, "I have accomplished so much. Why don't I feel more proud of myself?"

Although there are several reasons why someone may not enjoy his or her achievements, it can be useful to ask, "Who *chose* your goals? You — or the voice of some 'significant other' inside you?" Neither pride nor self-esteem can be supported by the pursuit of second-hand values that do not reflect who we really are.

Volitional Choice: What We Are Willing To Do
· · · · · · · · · · · ·

As far as our own actions and behavior are concerned, our self-esteem depends, to a very great extent, on what we are willing to do.

I stress this aspect of volitional choice because there is reason to believe that we may come into this world with certain inherent differences that may make it easier or harder to attain healthy self-esteem — differences pertaining to energy, resilience, disposition to enjoy life, and the like. I suspect that in future years we will learn that our genetic inheritance is definitely part of the story.

And certainly upbringing can play a powerful role. No one can say how many individuals suffer such damage in the early years before the psyche is fully formed, that it is all but impossible for healthy self-esteem to emerge later, short of intense psychotherapy.

Research suggests that one of the best ways to have good self-esteem is to have parents who have good self-esteem and who model it, as is made clear in Stanley Coopersmith's *The Antecedents Of Self-Esteem*. In addition, if we have parents who raise us with love and respect, who allow us to experience consistent and benevolent acceptance, who give us the supporting structure of reasonable rules and appropriate expectations, who do not assail us with contradictions, who do not resort to ridicule, humiliation, or physical abuse as means of controlling us, who project that they believe in our competence and goodness — we have a decent chance of internalizing their attitudes and thereby acquiring the foundation for healthy self-esteem.

But no research study has ever found this result to be inevitable. Coopersmith's study, for one, clearly shows that it is not. There are people who appear to have been raised superbly by the standards indicated above, and yet who are insecure, self-doubting adults. And there are people who have emerged from appalling backgrounds, raised by adults who did everything wrong, yet they do well in school, form stable and satisfying relationships, have a powerful sense of their own value and dignity, and as adults satisfy any rational criterion of good self-esteem. It is as if they were put on earth to baffle and confound psychologists.

While we may not know all the biological or developmental factors that influence self-esteem, we know a good deal about the specific (volitional) practices that can raise or lower it. We know that an honest commitment to understanding inspires self-trust and that an avoidance of the effort has the opposite effect. We know that people who live mindfully feel more competent than those who live mindlessly. We know that integrity engenders self-respect and that hypocrisy does not. We *know* all this implicitly, although it is astonishing how rarely such matters are discussed.

Supporting Self-Esteem
. . . .

We cannot work on self-esteem directly, neither our own nor anyone else's, because self-esteem is *a consequence* — a product of internally generated practices — such as that of living consciously, responsibly, purposefully, and with integrity. If we understand what those practices are, we can commit to *initiating* them within ourselves and to dealing with others in such a way as to *facilitate* or *encourage* them to do likewise. To encourage self-esteem in the family, the school, or the workplace, for instance, is to create an environment that supports and reinforces the practices that strengthen self-esteem.

How Does Healthy Self-Esteem Manifest?

There are some fairly simple and direct ways in which healthy self-esteem manifests itself in our being. These include:

- A face, manner, way of talking and moving that project the pleasure one takes in being alive.

- Ease in talking of accomplishments or shortcomings with directness and honesty, since one is in friendly relationship to facts.

- Comfort in giving and receiving compliments, expressions of affection, appreciation, and the like.

- Open to criticism and comfortable about acknowledging mistakes because one's self-esteem is not tied to an image of "perfection."

- One's words and movements tend to have a quality of ease and spontaneity since one is not at war with oneself.

- Harmony between what one says and does and how one looks, sounds and moves.

- An attitude of openness to and curiosity about new ideas, new experiences, new possibilities of life.

- Feelings of anxiety or insecurity, if they present themselves, will be less likely to intimidate or overwhelm one, since accepting them, managing them and rising above them rarely feels impossibly difficult.

- An ability to enjoy the humorous aspects of life, in oneself and others.

- Flexible in responding to situations and challenges, moved by a spirit of inventiveness and even playfulness, since one trusts one's mind and does not see life as doom or defeat.

- Comfort with assertive (not belligerent) behavior in oneself and others.

- Ability to preserve a quality of harmony and dignity under conditions of stress.

Then, on the purely physical level, one can observe characteristics such as these:

- Eyes that are alert, bright, and lively.

- A face that is relaxed and (barring illness) tends to exhibit natural color and good skin vibrancy.

- A chin that is held naturally and in alignment with one's body.

- A relaxed jaw.

- Shoulders relaxed yet erect.

- Hands that tend to be relaxed, graceful, and quiet.

- Arms tend to hang in a relaxed, natural way.

- Posture tends to be relaxed, erect, well-balanced.

- A walk that tends to be purposeful (without being aggressive and overbearing).

- Voice tends to be modulated with an intensity appropriate to the situation, and with clear pronunciation.

Notice that the theme of relaxation occurs again and again. Relaxation implies that we are not hiding from ourselves and are not at war with who we are. Chronic tension conveys a message of some form of internal split, some form of self-avoidance or self-repudiation, some aspect of the self being disowned or held on a very tight leash.

I asked a variety of psychotherapists of different theoretical orientations by what fairly simple criteria they would intuit a client's self-esteem. Interestingly, there was a high level of agreement among us.

How Much Is Enough Self-Esteem?
. . . .

Is it possible to have too much self-esteem?

No, it is not; no more than it is possible to have too much physical health. Sometimes self-esteem is confused with boasting or bragging or arrogance, but such traits reflect, not too much self-esteem, but too little. They reflect a lack of self-esteem. People of high self-esteem are not driven to make themselves superior to others; they do not seek to prove their value by measuring themselves against a comparative standard. Their joy is in being who they are, not in being better than someone else.

Engendering Resentment In The Less Secure
. . . .

True enough, people with troubled self-esteem are often uncomfortable in the presence of high self-esteem people and they may even feel resentful and declare, "They have *too much* self-esteem."

Insecure men, for instance, often feel more insecure in the presence of self-confident women. Low self-esteem individuals often feel irritable in the presence of people who are enthusiastic about life. If one partner in a marriage, whose self-esteem is deteriorating, sees that the partner's self-esteem is growing, the response is sometimes anxiety and an attempt to abort the growth process.

The sad truth is, whoever is successful in this world runs the risk of being a target. People of low achievement often envy and resent people of high achievement. Those who are unhappy often envy and resent those who are happy. Those of low self-esteem sometimes like to talk about the danger of having "too much self-esteem."

4

Reflections On The Sources Of Self-Esteem

. . . .

I remember as a child being enormously bewildered by the behavior of adults, by what I perceived as the strangeness and superficiality of their values, by the lack of congruence between statements and feelings, by an anxiety that seemed to saturate much of the atmosphere around me, and by the overwhelming sense that often the adults did not know what they were doing, that they were lost and helpless while pretending to be in control. This experience was painful and at times frightening. I desperately wanted to understand why human beings behaved as they did. Somewhere in my mind, at quite a young age, there must have been the conviction that knowledge is power, safety, security, and serenity. Doubtless this conviction played a significant role in my choice of profession.

51

All of us know times of bewilderment, despair, and a painful sense of impotence or inadequacy. The question is: *Do we allow such moments to define us?*

It's not that people of healthy self-esteem do not suffer or sometimes know anxiety. But they are not stopped by such experiences. They do not identify themselves with their fear or pain, just as, if they got sick, they would not identify themselves with their sickness. They do not see suffering as the essence of life.

Living Consciously, Responsibly, With Integrity
. . . .

The need for self-esteem arises from the fact that the function of our consciousness is volitional, which confers upon us a unique task — that of making ourselves competent to cope with the challenges of life. We achieve this by living consciously, responsibly, and with integrity.

We should judge ourselves by that which is in our volitional control, as I have already stressed. To judge ourselves by that which depends on the will and choices of others is clearly dangerous to our self-esteem. The tragedy of millions of people is that this is just what they do.

Self-esteem pertains to the issue of our fundamental appropriateness to life and, therefore, to the mental operations that lie behind our behavior. If this is understood, we can readily appreciate the error of measuring our worth by such standards as our popularity, influence, affluence, material possessions, or good looks.

Since we are social beings, some measure of esteem from others is necessary. But to tie our self-assessment to the good opinion of others is to place ourselves at their mercy in the most humiliating way. The desire to "please" (and to avoid disapproval) can lead us to do things that *betray* our self-esteem. And what are we to do when the people whose esteem we desire have different expectations, so that to gain the approval of one of our significant others is to risk the disapproval of another?

Or again, we may take pleasure in an attractive appearance, but to tie our self-esteem to our appearance is to be in growing terror with every passing year as the marks of age inevitably advance upon us. And if our good looks are far superior to our behavior, they will hardly heal the psychic wounds inflicted by dishonesty, irresponsibility, or irrationality.

A Commitment To Awareness: The Will To Understand
. . . .

Whenever we see men and women of high self-esteem, we see a high commitment to awareness as a way of life. They live *mindfully*.

They are concerned to know what they are doing when they act, to understand themselves and the world around them — including the feedback they receive, which informs them whether they are on- or off-course with regard to their goals and purposes.

In *Honoring the Self,* I call this attitude "the will to understand."

The potential range of our awareness depends on the extent of our intelligence, on the breadth of our abstract capacity, which means our ability to grasp relationships (to see the connection between things). But the principle of commitment to awareness, or the will to understand, remains the same on all levels of intelligence. It entails the behavior of seeking to integrate that which enters our mental field — as well as the effort to keep expanding that field.

The beginning of self-assertion is the assertion of consciousness itself, the act of seeing and of seeking to grasp that which we see, of hearing and of seeking to grasp that which we hear — or responding to life actively rather than passively. This is the foundation of good self-esteem.

The Bewildering World Of Adults
. . . .

Many children undergo experiences that place enormous obstacles in the way of the healthy development of this attitude. A child may find the world of parents and other adults incomprehensible and threatening. The self is not nurtured but attacked. After a number of unsuccessful attempts to understand adult policies, statements, and behavior, some children give up—and take the blame for their feelings of helplessness. Often they sense, miserably, desperately, and inarticulately, that there is something terribly wrong — with their elders, or with themselves, or with *something*. What they often come to feel is: "I'll never understand people; I'll never be able to do what they expect of me; I don't know what's right or wrong, and I'm never going to know."

Developing A Powerful Source Of Strength
. . . .

The child who continues to struggle to make sense out of the world and the people in it, however, is developing a powerful source of strength, no matter what the anguish of bewilderment experienced. Caught in a particularly cruel, frustrating, and irrational environment, he or she will doubtless feel alienated from many of the people in the immediately surrounding world, and legitimately so. But the child will not feel alienated from reality, will not feel, at the deepest level, incompetent to live — or at least he or she has a relatively good chance to avoid this fate.

The growing individual who retains a commitment to awareness learns subjects, acquires skills, accomplishes tasks — reaches goals. And of course these successes validate and reinforce the choice to think. The sense of being appropriate to life feels natural.

A commitment to awareness, then — a commitment to rationality, consciousness, respect for reality, as a way of life — is both a source and an expression of positive self-esteem.

Often we associate positive self-esteem only with the result — with knowledge, success, the admiration and appreciation of others — and miss the cause: all the choices that, cumulatively, add up to what we call a commitment to awareness, the will to understand. We thus can deceive ourselves about the actual sources of self-esteem.

The Will To Be Efficacious
. . . .

Where we see self-esteem, we see what I call "the will to be efficacious."

The concept of the will to be efficacious is an extension of the will to understand. It places its emphasis on the aspect of perseverance in the face of difficulties: continuing to seek understanding when understanding does not come easily; pursuing the mastery of a skill or the solution to a problem in the face of defeats; maintaining a commitment to goals while encountering many obstacles along the way.

The will to be efficacious is the refusal to identify our ego or self with momentary feelings of helplessness and defeat.

Many years ago I witnessed an encounter between two colleagues, a psychologist and a psychiatrist, which was important for my own understanding of the issue I am discussing. The two men were first cousins and had grown up in similar environments. They shared many painful memories of the behavior of their elders and other relatives.

"You survived all that in a way I didn't," the psychiatrist said to the psychologist. "They didn't get to you. I always wondered what made you persevere. Because I didn't. I gave up in some way."

The psychologist answered, "I do recall feeling quite overwhelmed many times. But somewhere deep in my body was a voice saying, 'Don't give up. Hang on.' Hang on to staying conscious, I suppose. Hang on to trying to understand. Don't give up the conviction that it's possible to be in control of your life. Obviously those weren't the words I used as a child, but that was the meaning. That's what I clung to."

"The will to be efficacious," I volunteered impulsively. The will to be efficacious — here was a concept that helped me explain something I had observed in my clients and students, the principle to help understand the difference between those who felt fundamentally defeated by life and those who did not.

The will to be efficacious — *the refusal of a human consciousness to accept helplessness as its permanent and unalterable condition.*

"Strategic Detachment"
Knowing You Are More Than Your Problems
. . . .

It is impressive to see a person who has been battered by life in many ways, who is torn by a variety of unsolved problems, who may be alienated from many aspects of the self — and yet who is still fighting, still struggling, still striving to find the path to a more fulfilling existence, moved by the wisdom of knowing, "I am more than my problems."

Children who survive extremely adverse childhoods have learned a particular survival strategy that relates to the issue we are discussing. I call it "strategic detachment." This is not the withdrawal from reality that leads to psychological disturbance, but rather an intuitively calibrated *disengagement* from noxious aspects of their family life or other aspects of their world. They somehow know, *This is not all there is.* They hold the belief that a better alternative exists *somewhere* and that *some day they will find their way to it.* They persevere in that idea. They somehow know *Mother is not all women, Father is not all men, this family does not exhaust the possibilities of human relationships — there is life beyond this neighborhood.* This does not spare them suffering in the present, but it allows them not to be destroyed by it. Their strategic detachment does not guarantee that they will never know feelings of powerlessness, but it helps them not to be stuck there.

Whether as children or adults, having the will to be efficacious does not mean that we deny or disown feelings of inefficacy when they arise. It means that we do not accept them as permanent. We feel temporarily helpless without defining our essence as helplessness. We can feel temporarily defeated without defining our essence as failure. We can allow ourselves to feel temporarily hopeless, overwhelmed, while preserving the knowledge that after a rest, we will pick up the pieces as best we can and start moving forward again. Our vision of our life extends beyond the feelings of the moment. Our concept of self can rise above today's adversity. This is one of the forms of heroism possible to a volitional consciousness.

Self-Esteem And IQ

. . . .

No study has ever suggested that good self-esteem correlates with IQ. And this is not surprising. Self-esteem is a function, not of our native endowment, but of our manner of using our consciousness — the choices we make concerning awareness, the honesty of our relationship to reality, the level of our personal integrity.

Self-esteem is neither competitive nor comparative. Its context is always the individual's relationship to self and to the choices of self. A person of high intelligence and high self-esteem does not feel *more* appropriate to life or *more* worthy of happiness than a person of high self-esteem and more modest intelligence.

An analogy may prove helpful. Two people may be equally healthy and physically fit, but one is stronger than the other. The one who is stronger does not experience a higher level of physical well-being; one can merely do some things the other cannot. Looking at them from the outside, we may say that one enjoys certain advantages over the other. But this does not mean that there is a difference in the internal feeling of wellness and aliveness.

Thinking Independently

. . . .

Intellectual independence is implicit in the commitment
to awareness or the will to understand. A person cannot
think through the mind of another. We can learn from one
another, but knowledge entails understanding, not mere
repetition or imitation. We can either exercise our own
mind or pass on to others the responsibility of knowledge
and evaluation and accept their verdicts more or less un-
critically. The choice we make is crucial for the way we
experience ourselves and for the kind of life we create.

Goals And Intentions Are Crucial

. . . .

That we are sometimes influenced by others in ways
we do not recognize does not alter the fact that there is a
distinction between the psychology of those who try to
understand things for themselves, think for themselves,
judge for themselves, and those to whom such a possibility rarely occurs. What is crucial here is the matter of
intention, the matter of an individual's goal.

I recall a client in therapy once saying to me, "I can't
understand why I'm always relying on the opinions of
other people."

I asked her, "As you were growing up, did you ever *want*
to be independent — did you ever make independence
your goal?"

She pondered for a moment, then replied, "No."

I said, "No need to be surprised, then, that you didn't arrive there."

To speak of "thinking independently" is useful because the redundancy has value in terms of emphasis. Often what people call "thinking" is merely recycling the opinions of others. So we can say that thinking independently — about our work, our relationships, the values that will guide our life, the goals we will set for ourselves — is a generator of self-esteem. And healthy self-esteem results in a natural inclination to think independently.

Self-Esteem Is Acquired, Not Given

· · · · · · · · · · · ·

Seeing only the tail end of the process I am describing, a person might say, "It's easy for him to think independently. Look at how much self-esteem he has." But self-esteem is not a given; it is acquired.

One of the ways self-esteem is acquired is by thinking independently when it may not be easy to do so, when it may even be frightening, when the person doing the thinking is struggling with feelings of uncertainty and insecurity and is choosing to persevere nonetheless. It is not always easy to stand by our judgment, and if it has become easy, that itself is a psychological victory — because in the past there were certainly times when it was not easy, when the pressures against independent thought were considerable, and when we had to confront and endure anxiety.

When a child finds that his or her perceptions, feelings, or judgments conflict with those of parents or other family members, and the question arises of whether to heed the voice of self or to disown it in favor of the voice of others. When a woman believes that her husband is wrong on some fundamental issue, and the question arises of whether to express her thoughts or to suppress them and thus protect the "closeness" of the relationship. When an artist or scientist suddenly sees a path that would carry him or her far from the consensual beliefs and values of colleagues, far from the mainstream of contemporary orientation and opinion, and the question arises of whether to follow that lonely path wherever it leads or to draw back. The issue and the challenge in all such situations remain the same. Should one honor one's inner signals or disown them?

Independence versus conformity,

self-expression versus self-repudiation,

self-assertion versus self-surrender.

The Heroism Of Consciousness
· · · · · · · · · · · ·

While it may sometimes be necessary, we do not normally enjoy long periods of being alienated from the thinking and beliefs of those around us, especially those we respect and love. One of the most important forms of heroism is the heroism of consciousness, the heroism of thought; the willingness to tolerate aloneness.

Like every other psychological trait, independence is a matter of degree. Although no one is perfectly independent and no one is hopelessly dependent all of the time, the higher the level of our independence and the more willing we are to think for ourselves, the higher tends to be the level of our self-esteem.

Learning To Discriminate
. . . .

No one can feel properly efficacious (that is, competent to cope with the basic challenges of life) who has not learned to differentiate between facts on the one hand and wishes and fears on the other.

The task is sometimes difficult because thoughts themselves are invariably touched or even saturated with feeling. Still, on many occasions we can recognize that the desire to perform some action is not proof that we should perform it. Running out of the room in the midst of an argument when we become upset, for example. And the fact that we may be afraid to perform some action is not proof that we should avoid performing it. Going to a physician for a checkup when there are signs of illness is another example.

If we make a purchase we know we cannot afford and avoid thinking about impending bills we will not be able to pay, we have surrendered our consciousness to our wishes. If we ignore signs of danger in a marriage and then profess to be bewildered and dismayed when the marriage finally explodes, we have paid the penalty for sacrificing consciousness to fear.

Our Underlying Intention

· · · · · · · · · · · ·

As far as our self-esteem is concerned, the issue is not whether we are flawless in executing the task of distinguishing among facts, wishes, and fears and choosing consciousness over some form of avoidance. Rather, the issue is one of our underlying intention.

When we describe a person as "basically honest," in the sense meant here, we do not mean that he or she is impervious to the influence of the wishes and fears, but rather that there is a pronounced and evident *desire* and *intention* to see things as they are. We cannot always know for certain whether or not we are being rational or honest; but we can certainly be concerned about it, we can certainly care. We are not always free to succeed in our thinking, but we are always free to try.

The accumulated sum of our choices in this matter yields an inner sense of basic honesty or dishonesty — a fundamental responsibility or irresponsibility toward existence. From childhood on, some individuals are far more interested in and respectful of such questions of truth than others. Some operate as if facts need not be facts if we do not choose to acknowledge them, as if truth is irrelevant and lies are lies only if someone finds them out.

The task of consciousness is to perceive that which exists, to the best of our ability. To honor reality — the perception of that which exists — is to honor consciousness; to honor consciousness is to honor self-esteem.

Integrity

• • • • • • • • • • • •

Where we see self-esteem, we see behavior that is consistent with the individual's professed values, convictions, and beliefs. We see integrity.

When we behave in ways that conflict with our judgments of what is appropriate, we lose face in our own eyes. We respect ourselves less. If the policy becomes habitual, we trust ourselves less — or cease to trust ourselves at all.

In their eagerness to dissociate themselves from philosophy in general and ethics in particular, psychologists are often uncomfortable with anything that sounds like a reference to morality in the context of psychotherapy or psychological well-being. In consequence, they can miss the obvious fact that integrity is, in effect, one of the guardians of mental health and that it is cruel and misleading to encourage people to believe that practicing "unconditional positive regard" toward themselves will bring them to undiluted self-love, irrespective of the question of their personal integrity.

Values, Principles, And Standards
. . . .

Sometimes an individual seeks to escape from the burden of integrity by disavowing, or professing to disavow, all values and standards. The truth is, human beings cannot successfully regress to a lower level of evolution; we cannot draw back to a time before thinking in principles and long-range planning were possible. We are conceptual beings, that is our nature, and we cannot function successfully as anything less. We need values to guide our actions. We need principles to guide our lives. Our standards may be appropriate or inappropriate to the requirements of our life and well-being, but to live without standards of any kind is impossible. So profound a rebellion against our nature as the attempt to discard all values, principles, and standards is itself an expression of impoverished self-esteem and a guarantee the impoverishment will be ongoing.

Let us acknowledge that the issue of living up to our standards is not always simple. What if our standards are mistaken or irrational?

A Code Of Values
. . . .

We may accept a code of values that does violence to our needs as living organisms. For example, certain religious teachings implicitly or explicitly damn sex, damn pleasure, damn the body, damn ambition, damn material success, damn (for all practical purposes) the enjoyment of life on earth. This acceptance of life-denying standards is an enormous problem and one I have written about in *The Psychology of Self-Esteem* and *Honoring the Self*.

Here, I will simply observe that once we see that living up to our standards appears to be leading us toward self-destruction, the time has obviously come to question our standards, rather than simply resigning ourselves to living without integrity. We may need to summon up the courage to challenge some of our deepest assumptions concerning what we have been taught to regard as the good.

Self-Acceptance
· · · · · · · · · · · ·

Where we see self-esteem, we see self-acceptance. High self-esteem individuals tend to avoid falling into an adversarial relationship with themselves.

If we are to grow and change, we must begin by learning self-acceptance. In my experience, self-acceptance is not an easy concept for most people to understand. (In *How to Raise Your Self-Esteem*, the longest chapter is devoted to this issue.) The tendency is to equate self-acceptance with the approval of every aspect of our personality (or physical appearance) and with the denial that any change or improvement might be desirable.

To be self-accepting does not mean to be without a wish to change, improve, evolve. It means not to be at war with ourselves — not to deny the reality of what is true of us right now, at this moment of our existence. We deal here with the issue of respect for and acceptance of the facts — in this case, the facts of our own being.

To accept ourselves is to accept the fact that what we think, feel, and do are all expressions of the self *at the time they occur.* So long as we cannot accept the fact of what we are at any given moment of our existence, so long as we cannot permit ourselves fully to be aware of the nature of our choices and actions, cannot admit the truth into our consciousness, we cannot change.

Accepting what I am requires that I approach the contemplation of my own experience with an attitude that makes the concepts of approval or disapproval irrelevant: *the desire to be aware.*

Unconditional Self-Acceptance
. . . .

There is still a deeper level on which we need to understand self-acceptance. Self-acceptance, in the ultimate sense, refers to an attitude of self-value and self-commitment that derives fundamentally from the fact that I am alive and conscious. It is deeper than self-esteem. It is a prerational, premoral act of self-affirmation — a kind of primitive egoism that is the birthright of every conscious organism. Yet, human beings have the power to act against or nullify this deep self-affirmation.

An attitude of self-acceptance is precisely what an effective psychotherapist appeals to or strives to awaken in a person of even the lowest self-esteem. This attitude can inspire a person to face whatever he or she most dreads to encounter within, without collapsing into self-hatred, repudiating the value of his or her person, or surrendering the will to live. Thus a person might be unhappy about experiencing poor self-esteem, yet accept it along with the self-doubts and feelings of guilt. "I accept them as part of how I experience myself right now."

Self-acceptance, at this level, is unconditional. Self-esteem is not, and cannot be.

When I endeavor to communicate the concept of self-acceptance to clients in therapy, I am sometimes met with protests. "But I don't *like* the way I am. I want to be different." Or, "I see people I admire — people who are strong, confident, assertive. That's the way I want to be. Why should I accept being a nonentity?"

We can note here the two fallacies already mentioned: the belief that if we accept who and what we are, we must approve of everything about us, and the belief that if we accept who and what we are, we are indifferent to change or improvement.

Self-Acceptance Facilitates Change
. . . .

I recall a female client who insisted that she could not possibly feel anything but self-loathing because of her inability to refuse any man's sexual overtures. I asked her if it was really true that she saw herself as a woman who could not say no. "Yes," she replied tearfully. I asked her if she was willing to accept that fact. "I hate it!" she replied.

I said that since it was true that was how she saw herself, was she willing to accept that truth and acknowledge it? After some initial reluctance she said, "I accept the fact that I see myself as a woman who can't say no."

When I asked her how saying that made her feel, she replied, "Angry."

Then I asked her if she could accept the fact that she feels very angry when she acknowledges perceiving herself as a woman who can't say no.

She said indignantly, "I *refuse* to accept the fact that I am that kind of person!"

I asked her, "Then how can you ever hope to change?"

I guided her through several psychological exercises aimed at facilitating her acceptance of her present state. Essentially they consisted of helping her experience that this was the way she was *right now*. After a while, she reported a change of feeling; she gave up the sense of fighting herself. She began relaxing into the feeling that "at this time in my life, this is part of who I am."

"This is so strange," she remarked. "Nothing has changed. I still have the problem. But I feel calmer. I've stopped shouting at myself. It's just . . . a fact about me. I don't like it, but it's a fact. I acknowledge it. Not just with words, but, you know, really accepted as true. Nothing has changed, and yet I feel as if I have more self-respect."

Then she made the most significant statement. "And as I begin to accept the reality of what I've been doing, how I've been living, it seems as if it would be much harder to go on doing it — I mean, to go on doing things of which I disapprove. Things that are humiliating. Perhaps that's why I've resisted accepting it. As soon as you stop fighting and accept, something begins to happen."

The Power Of Self-Responsibility
· · · · · · · · · · ·

Working with clients in psychotherapy, I am intrigued by catching the moment at which growth suddenly seems to spurt forward. I often see that the most radical transformation occurs after the client's realization that *no one is coming to the rescue.* "When I finally allowed myself to face fully my own responsibility for my life," more than one client has said to me, "I began to grow. I began to change. And my self-esteem began to rise."

In reality, we are responsible for our choices and actions. Not responsible as the recipient of moral blame or guilt, but responsible as the chief causal agent in our lives and behavior.

I do not mean to imply that a person never suffers through accident or through the fault of others, nor that a person is responsible for everything in life that may happen to him or her. We are not omnipotent. But self-responsibility is clearly indispensable to good self-esteem. Avoiding self-responsibility victimizes us with regard to our own lives. It leaves us helpless. It is just this view from which many people need to emancipate themselves if they are ever to evolve to a nontragic sense of life.

There is self-empowerment in declaring (and meaning!):

"I am responsible for the attainment of my desires and goals."

"I am responsible for my choices and actions."

"I am responsible for how I deal with people."

"I am responsible for the level of consciousness and conscientiousness I bring to my work."

"I am responsible for the decisions by which I live."

"I am responsible for my personal happiness."

Much more remains to be said about the conditions of successful self-esteem — more than can be covered in this book. What I have offered here are some general observations concerning the fundamentals.

The Roots Of Self-Esteem Are Internal
. . . .

Self-esteem is rooted internally — in mental operations — rather than in external successes or failures. This is an essential point to understand.

The failure to understand this principle causes an incalculable amount of unnecessary anguish and self-doubt. If we judge ourselves by criteria that entail factors outside our volitional control, the result, unavoidably, is a precarious self-esteem that is in chronic jeopardy. But our self-esteem need not be affected or impaired if, in spite of our best efforts, we fail in a particular undertaking, even though we will not experience the same emotion of pride that we would have felt if we had succeeded.

Further, we need to remember that the self is not a static, finished entity, but a continually evolving creating, an unfolding of our potentialities, expressed in our choices, decisions, thoughts, judgments, responses, and actions. To view ourselves as basically and unalterably good or bad — independent of our present and future manner of functioning — is to negate the facts of freedom, self-determination, and self-responsibility. We always contain within ourselves the possibility of change.

We need never be the prisoner of yesterday's choices.

5

The Power Of Self-Esteem In The Workplace

Self-esteem may be the most important psychological resource we have to help us meet the challenges of the future. That challenge is especially evident in the workplace where it is becoming clear that self-esteem is not an emotional luxury but a survival requirement.

Recent research is helping to clarify the important role that self-esteem plays in our ability to take risks, learn new skills, be creative, take feedback, deal with others fairly and benevolently, be productive and assertive. We need to cultivate these important traits in order to function optimally in our families, organizations and communities.

Chapter adapted from an interview with Nathaniel Branden by Eryn J. Kalish in *Networking Magazine*, © 1991, Massachusetts Chapter of the American Society for Training & Development.

We have reached a moment in history when self-esteem, which has always been a supremely important psychological survival need, has now become a supremely important economic survival need as well.

We have witnessed the shift from a manufacturing society to an information society — and from a domestic economy to a global economy. We live in a time of extraordinarily rapid change, of phenomenal scientific and psychological breakthrough. Muscle-work is becoming a smaller and smaller part of our economic activity; mind-work is on the rise. This is the day of the knowledge-worker. New management techniques must be developed that are appropriate for managing a better educated, more independent and creative workforce. Even psychotherapists and counselors need greater awareness of these issues as they see more clients with job-related stress.

Developments in the workplace in this time of accelerating change, choices, and challenges demand a greater capacity for innovation, self-management, personal responsibility and self-direction — all qualities of high self-esteem.

Trusting Yourself
. . . .

The most fundamental meaning of self-esteem is trust in your own mind, your own mental processes. Therefore, trust in your ability to learn, to judge, to decide. So, the primary way we can think of self-esteem as a survival need is in the context of realizing that for humans, the mind, or consciousness, is the basic means of survival on which we rely to keep us in contact with reality and guide our behavior appropriately.

An individual who at a core level distrusts his or her own mind is severely disadvantaged in coping with the choices and options that life presents.

Think of positive self-esteem as the immune system of consciousness, providing resistance, strength and a capacity for regeneration in handling the challenges of life.

The Ability To Make Decisions

Studies conducted among top executives suggest that one of the leading causes of failure is the inability to make decisions. That inability is due to troubled self-esteem — distrusting one's own mind and judgment.

In many situations, a great amount of information must be obtained and analyzed in order for managers to make good decisions, and certainly the input of others is a contributing factor. Much has been written about the value of making "balanced" decisions, but that must mean more than merely gathering votes. Consensus-thinking may actually lead away from innovative choices.

Guidelines For Making Decisions

In my view, decision-making is a matter of looking at the widest possible context when you make your decisions. Of asking yourself:

1. What are all of the factors I know of that can
   conceivably bear upon my decision?
2. What are all of the foreseeable consequences of
   my decision?
3. Who is likely to be affected and how?

In other words, a highly conscious person is looking for
the greatest amount of relevant input that he or she can
find to guide the decision-making process. It is not a matter
of my decision versus someone else's. It is an issue of respect for fact, respect for truth. One of the hallmarks of
healthy self-esteem is a strong reality orientation — and
then trusting your own mind to make the right decision.

There will be contexts in which healthy self-esteem
includes or even demands getting input from others,
though that does not necessarily mean taking opinion
polls. Someone may be far ahead of the other people involved and able to see things others are not able to see.
The Wright brothers, for example, did not bother to take
a poll.

The consensus model of decision-making has its place,
but depends to some extent on the ability of innovators or
visionaries to get their ideas across. Some are not able to
articulate the vision clearly enough to get support for
what might be the best decision. Some very important
ideas are lost to this inability.

For an innovator to put across the new product or technique or management method, a high level of self-esteem
is of inestimable value.

Approaching Others In A Benevolent Spirit

· · · · · · · · · · ·

People who are happy to be themselves, who trust themselves, and are at peace with themselves, are free emotionally and psychologically to approach others in a benevolent spirit. Those with positive self-esteem tend to elicit cooperation, shared enthusiasm and consensus more readily than people who are more self-doubting, insecure and think in terms of a you versus me, win/lose model of human relationships.

Whether you are thinking about people in the context of a large organization or in their personal lives, people who trust themselves tend to deal with others with much greater respect and benevolence than those who do not, with predictable outcomes in terms of their ability to get consensus.

The Conviction That We Are Worthy Of Success

· · · · · · · · · · ·

This also relates to the worthiness component of self-esteem — that conviction that we are worthy and deserving of success, happiness, trust, respect and love.

All of life consists of pursuing values. To pursue values, I have to value the beneficiary of my values, namely myself. If at the core I don't feel worthy of success or happiness, I most likely will not attain it, and if I do I am unlikely to enjoy it. We often see people at work who feel capable but not worthy. So they work and work and never feel entitled to rest and enjoy what they have done.

People who doubt their efficacy and worth tend to experience fear of other people and, as a consequence, may tend to fall into adversarial relationships with them. These people are perceived as a threat.

If, in contrast, we have confidence in our efficacy and worth, we are much less likely to fall into a "you versus me" mentality. We are more likely to form cooperative relationships and to be skillful at building consensus.

High Levels Of Social Cooperation
. . . .

Allan S. Watterman, a New Jersey psychologist, did a comprehensive review of all the literature that exists about social cooperation and how well it correlates with a highly developed individuality. He found that it correlated very positively and not only with social cooperation but with the qualities of benevolence, generosity and compassion.

People with high self-esteem are not driven to make themselves superior to others; they do not seek to prove their value by measuring themselves against a comparative standard. Their joy is in being who they are, not in being better than someone else.

Feeling As If You Make A Difference
. . . .

I once worked with a rather unproductive team. One of the core causes was that many of the individuals on that team really didn't feel they could make a difference. They didn't think that their contribution was going to count at all. The more they began to believe their input would matter, the more easily they cooperated with each other. It was clearly an issue of self-esteem.

It is a basic human desire to be visible to others, to be seen and appreciated for who we are. And it is natural to want to work in an environment which supports us, supports our self-esteem, supports the view that our contribution can and will make a difference.

As economic cycles change, there are periods when people are unemployed or fear that they will be. Trying times can be handled better by those whose self-esteem and feelings of competence and self-worth are not derived exclusively from their jobs.

Competence: Internal, Security
• • • • • • • • • • • •

What I mean by competence is the internal security that comes from trusting your own mental processes, not from basing your feelings of self-worth on results which do not always depend only on yourself.

Many years ago I gave a self-esteem seminar in Detroit when the government was still in the process of deciding whether or not to bail out Chrysler. There were a number of Chrysler executives in the course and I said to them: "Here is what is wrong with basing your self-esteem on performance per se or income earning ability per se. Right now some people you don't even know are trying to decide whether or not to bail out Chrysler. Does it make sense that you are willing to place your self-esteem in their hands? If the idea offends you, good; it offends me. It doesn't make any kind of sense that your self-esteem should be at the mercy of factors over which you have absolutely no control."

It is a very difficult concept for many people to accept and understand. For men in our culture, and increasingly for women, having worth is tied up with having a paycheck or a job where you do something well.

Self-Esteem Anchored In Our Ability To Learn
. . . .

Because knowledge is exploding so rapidly, all of us, to remain effective, need to have a commitment to lifelong learning. For many, this represents a significant shift in attitude. It is not easy to take a more abstract approach in which self-esteem is anchored not in what we have or know but in our ability to learn. This is important not only in unstable economic times. *Any* unpredictable change can force the need to learn something new and a person should think in terms of his or her own processes, not skills per se.

For example, it is more helpful to ask, "how did I go from knowing nothing about engineering (or sales, or training, etc. . . .) to knowing quite a bit about it? What do I already know about learning unfamiliar things that I can bring to this new challenge?"

High Expectations For Success
. . . .

Those in a position to coach or train others need to cultivate an appreciation for the ability to learn. In the workplace, managers need to uphold high expectations for success in themselves and in those they manage and at the same time create an environment where it's safe to make responsible mistakes. It is very tricky to create a disciplined, risk-taking, non-punitive environment. Holding people to high levels of expectancy while allowing them to grow and learn is not a contradiction, but it does take a lot of careful thinking in order to implement.

You might start with the premise that they are going to have something worthwhile and interesting to say. And if you don't really believe that the person can think and that their opinion is worth something, think about how you would act if you *did* believe it. And then practice those behaviors for 30-60 days and notice any changes that occur.

Regarding setting high expectations, when delegating work, ask the person if they can accomplish this task, if they are willing to be responsible for delivering it, etc. Work to get firm agreement about what has been promised. And then review it after the task is done.

Goal-Setting Responsibility
. . . .

Whenever possible, it's desirable to have a group set its own expectations and goals within the framework of the organization's goals. It strengthens the experience of personal autonomy. And some research says that when groups set their own goals they tend to set them higher than when others set the goals for them.

Managers with positive self-esteem have less trouble giving up control of goal-setting and other tasks. To implement such management techniques as shared goal setting it is probably worthwhile to bring in a self-esteem expert who can really make clear what kind of difference it will make in the workplace and why.

Initially, self-esteem training seminars are helpful with the goal toward integrating the information into daily practices. Once people understand how self-esteem operates in the human psyche, they will spot opportunities for application that an outsider would not.

A manager is not a psychotherapist, and can't be expected to be. It has never been my view that managers should be. And furthermore, employees don't sign on for their manager's psychotherapy even if the manager were so disposed.

Challenge, Stimulate, And Stretch
. . . .

Studies suggest that we get the best out of people when we ask a little more of them than they think they can do.

In other words, we stretch them. We set our sights high, but not so high as to be paralyzing. I think the same principle can be applied to ourselves. Managers need to set their self-expectations realistically, to be sure, but high enough to challenge, stimulate and stretch. For every individual whose problem is that he overestimates his abilities, there are a hundred people who underestimate theirs.

If I were the CEO of an organization, I would put a lot of emphasis on cultivating in myself and my employees the knowledge that people can do all kinds of things they don't believe they can do. Positive expectancy can help people see beyond their own limitations. In training managers to help employees flourish, I would tell stories and give all kinds of examples hoping to spark the manager's creativity. This cannot be reduced to a training manual.

No Short-Cuts To Self-Esteem
. . . .

There really aren't any shortcuts to high self-esteem; we can't cheat reality. If we don't live consciously, authentically, responsibly, and with high integrity, we may be successful, popular, wealthy and belong to all the right clubs, but we will have only pseudo self-esteem. Self-esteem is always an intimate experience; it is what we think and feel about ourselves, not what someone else thinks and feels.

Self-esteem really is the reputation we get with ourselves.

6

Recommendations For Further Study

The central focus of my work as a psychologist has been the study of self-esteem, its role in human life, and, most particularly, its impact on work and love. If you have found the work you have just read of value, then the following works are suggested for further reading.

The Psychology of Self-Esteem. This is my first major theoretical exploration and overview of the entire field. Unlike my later books, it puts heavy emphasis on the philosophical foundations of my work. It deals with such questions as: What is self-esteem and why do we need it? Why is self-esteem such a powerful force in human life? What is the meaning — and justification — of the idea of free will? What is the relation of reason and emotion? How do rationality and integrity relate to self-esteem? Which moral values support self-esteem and which undermine it? Why is self-esteem the key to motivation?

Breaking Free. This is an exploration of the childhood origins of negative self-concepts, dramatized through a series of vignettes taken from my clinical practice. Through these stories we see in what ways adults can adversely affect the development of a child's self-esteem. Indirectly, therefore, the book is a primer on the art of child-rearing.

The Disowned Self. This book examines the painful and widespread problem of self-alienation, in which the individual is out of touch with his or her inner world, and indicates pathways to recovery. This book has proven especially helpful for adult children of dysfunctional families. It takes a fresh look at the relation of reason and emotion that goes beyond my earlier treatment of the subject in its scope and depth. Demonstrating how and why self-acceptance is essential to healthy self-esteem, it points the way to the harmonious integration of thought and feeling.

The Psychology Of Romantic Love. In this book I explore the nature and meaning of romantic love, its difference from other kinds of love, its historical development, and its special challenges in the modern world. It addresses such questions as: What love is. Why love is born. Why does it sometimes flourish? Why does it sometimes die?

What Love Asks of Us. Originally published as *The Romantic Love Question-and-Answer Book*, this revised and expanded edition, written with my wife and colleague, Devers Branden, addresses the questions we hear most often from those struggling with the practical challenges of making love work. It covers a wide range of topics, from the importance of autonomy in relationships, to the art of effective communication, to conflict-resolution skills, to dealing with jealousy and infidelity, to coping with the special challenges of children and in-laws, to surviving the loss of love.

Honoring the Self. Again returning to the nature of self-esteem and its role in our existence, this book is less philosophical than *The Psychology of Self-Esteem* and more developmental in its focus. It looks at how the self emerges, evolves, and moves through progressively higher stages of individuation. It explores what adults do that nourishes or subverts the growth of a child's positive sense of self — and what we as adults can do to raise the level of our own self-esteem. It examines the psychology of guilt. It addresses the relationship between self-esteem and productive work. It is the best summation of my thinking on self-esteem to date (1992).

If You Could Hear What I Cannot Say. This is a workbook. It teaches the fundamentals of my sentence-completion technique and how it can be used by a person working alone for self-exploration, self-understanding, self-healing, and personal growth.

The Art of Self-Discovery. This book carries the work of the preceding volume further. Originally published as *To See What I See and Know What I Know*, this revised and expanded edition aims to provide counselors and psychotherapists with tools to be utilized in their own clinical practice.

How To Raise Your Self-Esteem. The purpose here is to provide the reader with specific strategies for building self-esteem. The discussion is more concrete than in my earlier writings, more action-oriented. It is addressed equally to people working on their own development and to parents, teachers, and psychotherapists who are invited to experiment with the techniques it describes.

Judgment Day: My Years with Ayn Rand. This investigative memoir tells the story of my personal and intellectual development, including the rises and falls and rises of my own self-esteem, through my relationship with three women, of which the centerpiece is my relationship with novelist-philosopher Ayn Rand (*The Fountainhead, Atlas Shrugged*). It describes the extraordinary contexts in which I came upon some of my most important psychological ideas, including my first understanding, at the age of twenty-four, of the supreme importance of self-esteem to human well-being.

I am now at work on a major study of the foundations of healthy self-esteem. The new book, entitled *The Six Pillars of Self-Esteem* (to be published by Bantam Books in 1993), will explore the most important internal and external factors that contribute to and support healthy self-esteem. By "internal" I mean factors residing within, or generated by, the individual — ideas or beliefs, practices or behaviors. By "external" I mean factors in the environment: messages verbally or non-verbally transmitted, or experiences evoked, by parents, "significant others," teachers, organizations, and culture. I shall examine self-esteem from the inside and the outside: what is the contribution of the individual to his or her self-esteem and what is the contribution of other people? I regard this book as the climax of a lifetime of studying self-esteem.

All of these books are published by Bantam Books, with the exception of *Judgment Day*, which is published in hardcover by Houghton-Mifflin and in softcover by Avon.

Through the Branden Institute for Self-Esteem in Los Angeles, we offer psychotherapy and family counseling; conduct on-going self-esteem groups; give lectures, seminars, and workshops; create self-esteem/high performance programs for organizations; and do telephone consulting with individual and corporate clients.

For information, write to:

The Branden Institute for Self-Esteem
P.O. Box 2609
Beverly Hills, California 90213
Telephone: (310) 274-6361

Bednar, Richard L., et al., **Self-Esteem: Paradoxes & Innovations In Clinical Theory & Practice,** Washington, DC: American Psychological Association, 1989.

Branden, Nathaniel, **The Psychology Of Self-Esteem,** New York, NY: Bantam, 1971.

————, **Honoring The Self: The Psychology Of Confidence And Respect,** New York, NY: Bantam, 1983.

————, **How To Raise Your Self-Esteem,** New York, NY: Bantam, 1987.

Coopersmith, Stanley, **The Antecedents Of Self-Esteem,** 2nd Ed., Pala Alto, CA: Consulting Psychologists Pr. Inc., 1981.

James, William, **Principles Of Psychology,** 2 Vols., Cambridge, MA: Harvard University Press, 1983.

Toward A State Of Esteem; The Final Report Of The California Task Force To Promote Self-Esteem And Personal And Social Responsibility, Sacramento, CA: Bureau of Publications, California State Department of Education, 1990.